"Hey Tim," he called. "Let's pick some plums for Miss Foote and take them to her."

I frowned, thinking that it wasn't a good idea.

"They're not our plums," I said. "What's our teacher going to say if we turn up with stolen plums? She's not going to be happy."

"C'mon," Vincent smiled. "She won't mind. She's cool. She'll like it."

I wasn't sure, but I agreed.

MRS BATTLESHIP

First published by OneTree House Ltd, New Zealand, 2019

Text © Tim Tipene, 2019

978-0-9951067-9-6

Some names and identifying details have been changed to protect the privacy of individuals and the actions described are as the author remembers them.

All rights reserved. No part of this publication may be reproduced, stored in a retrieval system or transmitted in any form or by any means, electronic, mechanical, photocopying, recording or otherwise, without the prior permission of the publisher.

Cover design byMinky Stapleton

Illustrations by Carol Green

Printed in New Zealand

10 9 8 7 6 5 4 3 2   9/1   0 1 2 3/2

MRS BATTLESHIP

TIM TIPENE

OneTree
HOUSE

To the amazing teachers
who change lives – TT

CHAPTERS

WHO AM I?	5
BUTTERFLY TAPE	7
SCHOOL	15
MRS LEONARD	19
PLUMS FOR MISS	22
A SHORT STORY	29
THE BATTLESHIP	36
MRS BATTERSBY	41
MRS BATTERSBY RETIRES	50
DAD	54
MUM	60
I CHOSE A GOOD LIFE	64
RESPECT	67
CHOICE	70
HELPLINES	75
ABOUT THE AUTHOR	76

WHO AM I?

I am Tim Tipene, son, brother, father, writer, black belt ninja, leader of Warrior Kids, Kiwibank local hero and Inductee to the New Zealand Martial Arts Hall of Fame.

I am Māori, Ngāti Whātua, and Ngāti Kuri.

I am Pākehā, descendent of the Frost and Mead family lines from West Auckland.

I love my Mum and Dad. I love them very much, but when Mum and Dad were little they were both hurt, badly hurt. Then when they became adults and parents, they ended up hurting me, and my brothers and sister.

These are some of my stories.

BUTTERFLY TAPE

One afternoon my brother, Shaun, hit me. The two of us were home alone. He was eight and I was five. We had had an argument in my bedroom and he hit me. So I chased him.

Shaun ran through the house with me hot on his tail. He raced into his bedroom and slammed his glass door behind him just as my fist was coming down. My fist smashed through the glass. Shaun opened his door instantly and we both watched in horror as blood began to cover my arm. I was cut on the wrist, elbow and upper arm.

Seeing Shaun's fearful reaction, I too became scared. Clearly a plaster wasn't going to fix this. I started to cry.

Remembering that little cuts had to be washed, Shaun rushed me into the bathroom and had me put my arm under running water in the basin. But these cuts weren't little and the blood didn't stop running. Shaun turned the tap on full to see if that would help. The blood kept coming.

"Wait here," Shaun said. "I'm going to get Mrs Tantell."

"Are you coming back?" I asked.

"Yeah, yeah," he said, disappearing out the door.

I had visions of being left there as Shaun went off to play with his mates.

I watched a constant stream of my blood swirl around the basin and down the plughole. Our elderly neighbour, Mrs Tantell, came into the bathroom with Shaun. She wasted no time, taking my arm away from the tap and wrapping it firmly in a towel. She then picked me up, carried me outside and up Ferry Parade about 400 metres to a small private doctor's surgery.

Mrs Tantell pushed through the door and demanded to see the doctor right away. She explained what had happened and said that I needed urgent attention. However, the doctor was reluctant to see me. He was saying things about my family, saying that he wouldn't get paid. Mrs Tantell refused to leave.

The doctor wasn't happy. He had patients waiting. I was taken into his office and he looked me over.

"He's not going to die," he muttered.

"He needs stitches," Mrs Tantell said.

"I'm not doing stitches," the doctor argued. "I'll use butterfly tape."

"But the scarring will be worse with tape," Mrs Tantell said.

The doctor went ahead and taped up my cuts. A nurse followed putting my arm in bandages and a sling.

Mrs Tantell moaned about the doctor the whole time she was carrying me back down the road. When we got home Mum, Dad and little sister Katie had only just arrived. Shaun was helping them to take groceries out of the car and into the house. Mrs Tantell had a private word to Mum. Mum never liked Mr and Mrs Tantell. She said that they were nosy old buggers who should mind their own business.

After Mrs Tantell had left, Mum and Dad were open with their anger.

Mum said the only reason I wasn't getting a hiding was because of my arm. I was thankful.

I remember feeling angry at the doctor, angry because he had upset Mrs Tantell. She had only been trying to help.

Our house on Herald Island backed onto an inlet of the Waitemata Harbour and I used to watch that same doctor riding his pedal boat over the waves. It was a small barge with a bicycle on it. That doctor would get on there and peddle away, taking himself across the inlet. It was his regular exercise. I thought the pedal boat looked like fun. I fancied having a go myself. When I was 11 I did just that. I walked along the shore to the doctor's house and dragged his pedal boat down into the water. I climbed onto the bike and pedalled like crazy to make a quick getaway. I don't know how the doctor did it, but this boat was not quick at all. It took ages to get anywhere. I had only just started and I was already getting tired. But I persevered and kept going, taking the boat out into deeper water. When I looked back at the shore there was the doctor standing on the beach with his arms crossed.

"C'mon!" he yelled. "You've had your fun! Now bring it back!"

I stuck my head down and peddled harder trying to get away. But though I peddled madly the doctor was able to walk along the shoreline and keep up with me.

"You've got to come in some time!" he cried, advancing ahead of me on the beach.

"Stuff this," I thought.

The pedal boat was so slow that there was no escaping.

I turned the boat around and began the journey back into shore. It took forever and the whole time the doctor waited, walking along with me. I figured that I was going to be in trouble, but I had given up caring at this point of my life. Trouble came no matter what I did.

When I finally reached the shore the doctor was quick to get me off his pedal boat.

"What were you thinking, taking my boat?" he growled.

"I just wanted to have a go," I said.

"Then get your own boat," he snapped. "Don't be stealing other people's boats."

"I don't have any money," I explained.

"Then ask your parents to buy you one," he said.

"They're not going to buy me a boat," I argued.

"Well, stay away from mine!" he grumbled.

He threatened to phone the police. I was more worried about him phoning Mum and Dad. But he clearly wasn't brave enough to go to talk to them. Most people on Herald Island avoided talking to my parents.

"Stupid doctor," I thought as I walked away, remembering how he had treated me all those years before. As though I was a second-class citizen.

The butterfly tape was a helpful tip, though. Katie and I were doing handstands and cartwheels in the lounge one afternoon. I calculated wrong and ended up landing on Mum's fancy little coffee table. The table was all right, but my leg smashed her ornamental plate that had been on there. There was a big gash in my leg. I didn't need Mrs Tantell or the doctor this time, though. I knew that I could sort it myself. I got a towel and wrapped my leg up to stop the bleeding. Once it had stopped I got tape and wound it around my leg, keeping the cut together. Katie put the table back where it had been and we got rid of the evidence, hiding and later binning the broken plate and the bloodied towel.

We both knew what would happen to me if we got caught. I wore long pants for the next week to hide my leg. I didn't bath or shower. Now and then the wound would start bleeding. I used toilet paper to wipe it. Mum and Dad never noticed.

I still have the scars from my wounds. The scars on my arm remind me of Mrs Tantell. A true hero. She and her husband were both willing to confront my parents at different times, and brave the animosity. The scars on my leg remind me of my own ingenuity in a time when I was simply trying to survive. And it reminds me that there were many times that my younger sister, Katie, protected me.

SCHOOL

I didn't do well at school. I found school hard and confusing, and I found the work challenging. Yet school was one place where I felt safe. I didn't feel safe at home.

So 3 o'clock each day, when the last bell rang and school ended, I wanted to stay at school. I did not want to go home. Because I knew that when I went home someone was going to be angry, someone was going to fight, and someone was going to get hurt.

As much as I wanted to stay at school, though, I found the schoolwork hard and I always seemed to be doing the wrong thing. For example, on my first day, having no idea where the toilets were, I peed behind a small blackboard in the classroom.

"Miss, Miss," a horrified little girl cried, as she

pointed me out to the teacher and the rest of the class. The teacher was very upset with me.

Right from the beginning I was put into special classes for reading and for maths. Each morning would start with me sitting on the mat with the other children, and as the day got under way I would look out the classroom window and see a woman walking across the schoolyard. The woman would walk all the way into my classroom and there she would look at me.

"Timothy, come with me please," she would say.

She would take me across the school and into a little room, and in that little room she tried to help me with my maths and reading, because when it came to my learning I was behind all the other children.

This became the daily routine. Sit with all the other children and then be taken away. I knew this was because I was 'different'.

Sometimes I even had to go to the staffroom, and in the staffroom I had to work with a speech therapist. Her job was to help me to talk properly. So even in that I couldn't do as well as the other children. One thing that she helped me with was how to pronounce 'th' words correctly.

She would have me sit in front of her.

"Watch my tongue, Timothy," she would say, pointing at her mouth. "Watch my tongue."

Then she would say, "This, then, there, that," and I would have to repeat the words over and over again, making sure that I put my tongue in the right position and pronounced 'th' words correctly.

My first school was Hobsonville Primary, but I wasn't there long because the bus route changed. From then on I attended Whenuapai Primary. We were living in Ferry Parade on Herald Island in West Auckland at the time. Mum's parents had helped her buy a house there. Back then Herald Island wasn't the flash place it is today. All the properties had septic tanks and in the winter tanks would often over flow. The Island was a fun place to grow up, though, and there was always lots to do.

At school I wasn't always doing the right thing. However, I wouldn't say that I was a naughty child. I was a traumatised child because of the daily abuse and violence in my home.

Because I was being hurt every day I was in a

constant state of anxiety and fear, which meant I couldn't sit still or concentrate. I was constantly on the lookout for danger.

Being always on alert it was hard to focus on subjects like maths when I wasn't sure that I would still be alive the next day.

It also meant I turned into a scrapper. For me it was about survival and I didn't care how big or tough the other boys were.

On my first day at Whenuapai Primary School I was circled by a large group of older children and cheered on as I beat up a boy much bigger and older than me. Since others were egging me on I figured I must be doing the right thing. Stephen, my older brother Shaun's mate, even held my glasses while I got on with the job.

Shaun had tried to stop me fighting, but as I was being beaten at home I wanted to make certain that no one was going to hurt me at school. More than anything I wanted to be left alone and I thought this was the best way to achieve this.

MRS LEONARD

Some of my teachers knew about my life at home and went the extra mile to support me. There was no Ministry for Children in those days, so teachers found other ways to make my life easier.

One of my early teachers was Joan Leonard. Mrs Leonard would give me a kiss and a hug when I arrived at school each morning, and a kiss and a hug in the afternoon before I went home. It became my daily ritual and it helped me get through. Sadly this didn't last.

I was away from school for a while and when I returned I found that Mrs Leonard had left. She had been replaced by a new teacher. I studied the new teacher all day, wondering if the old arrangement still applied. Would I still get my kiss and hug at the beginning and end of each day? A couple of days passed before I actually picked up the courage to approach her. It was almost 3 o'clock and my classmates and I were in two lines. Boys in one line and girls in the other. We were waiting for the bell to ring for home time. The teacher stood in front, facing us.

It was now or never. I stepped out from the back of the line, walked up to the front, held out my arms and went in for a hug. The teacher stepped away from me as though I had leprosy.

"What are doing?" she frowned, looking me over.

I didn't know what to say.

My classmates spoke up for me.

"He wants a hug," a boy said.

"He always gets a hug," a girl added.

Their words were echoed by other students as they explained to the teacher that a kiss and hug is what Timothy was always given at the start and end of each day by Mrs Leonard.

"Well, I'm not having that!" the new teacher growled. She glared at me. "Get back into line."

Believe it or not, this is a happy memory. While

the teacher's reaction was disappointing and sad for me, it is the children's voices I hear the most. They had spoken up for me and I've never forgotten it.

As young children they had understood and accepted that I needed support. That I needed that bit extra. They had never questioned why I needed it, but they knew that I did, and they were more than okay with me getting it.

I am grateful to those children and to Mrs Leonard for the hugs and kisses. They really made a difference.

PLUMS FOR MISS

Year 6 / Standard 4

The principal at Whenuapai Primary liked to play the banjo, especially during school assemblies. Us students and the staff were his captive audience. In other words we couldn't leave. We all had to sit there and wait for him to finish belting out tune after tune. The principal would be up the front of the hall, jigging away as he played. He was having a great time. The teachers sat wearily in their seats on both sides of the hall. The performance was clearly as torturous for the staff as it was for us kids.

At the start of a new year the principal would announce the new teachers at the assembly. It was in such an assembly, following his banjo performance, that the principal introduced my new teacher.

"Miss Foote," he said, gesturing at a young woman sitting on the side.

The hall erupted with laughter.

"Where's Mr Hand?" someone yelled from the back.

The principal sorted out the laughter and chatter quickly with a stern condemnation of the disrespect. I could see that Miss Foote didn't like being laughed at. Her face was burning bright red.

Once we had left the hall and entered her classroom we got to see how genuine, warm and caring Miss Foote was. We all felt pretty stink for laughing at her name and no one dared do it again.

I fell in love with Miss Foote.

I was 10 years old, and I was going to marry her.

My friend Vincent turned up at my house one Saturday morning to tell me that our new teacher was living up the road from me.

I didn't believe him.

"Whatever," I said.

"She is," Vincent frowned.

I still wasn't convinced.

"Come on then, I'll show you!" Vincent growled.

"Okay!" I growled back.

So off we went.

We walked up Ferry Parade to the entrance of the Herald Island Domain. There Vincent led me to a two-storeyed, wooden house.

"This is it," he said.

We stood on the footpath, studying the house.

"Where is Miss Foote?" I asked.

"She must be inside," Vincent muttered.

"She doesn't live there," I said.

"She does," Vincent replied. "I saw her."

Vincent and I stayed watching the house, hoping to get a glimpse of Miss Foote, but we didn't see anyone. Our eyes drifted over to the adjacent property. There was no house on the section, just three plum trees standing tall. The trees were rich with bright red plums, ready for the picking.

Vincent and I looked at one another. We weren't going to miss out on those plums.

We jumped the fence and found our way through the long grass to the middle of the section. There we each scaled our own plum tree, munching on plums as we went. Our aim was to get to the top of the trees where the larger, riper plums shone in the sunlight, beckoning us.

After we had each gobbled down a number of plums Vincent looked from his tree to mine.

"Hey Tim," he called. "Let's pick some plums for Miss Foote and take them to her."

I frowned, thinking that it wasn't a good idea.

"They're not our plums," I said. "What's our teacher going to say if we turn up with stolen plums? She's not going to be happy."

"C'mon," Vincent smiled. "She won't mind. She's cool. She'll like it."

I wasn't sure, but I agreed.

We climbed down from the trees, turned our teeshirts over to make a pouch in the front and filled them up with ripe, red plums.

We then went through the fence into the backyard of the two storied, wooden house. I followed Vincent up the steps onto the back porch. He knocked on the door.

It wasn't long before we could hear footsteps moving through the house. I was thinking that this was probably a good time to run away.

Our teacher probably didn't live here at all. Chances were that the people who did live here were the owners of the plum trees next door. It wasn't going to look good us bringing them their own plums.

Vincent noticed me backing away.

"Nah, it's all good, man," he said. "It's our teacher's house. You wait and see."

The door opened and there she was. Miss Foote. She was surprised to see us.

"Good morning, boys," she smiled.

"We brought you some plums, Miss," Vincent announced.

We showed her the fruit in our pouches.

Miss Foote's eyes enlarged. This was it, I thought. Time for a lecture on not taking fruit that didn't belong to us.

"That's wonderful, boys," Miss Foote said.

She told us to wait as she went back inside. She soon returned with a bowl and got Vincent and I to tip our plums into it.

"Thank you, boys," Miss Foote beamed.

When Miss Foote smiled there was nowhere else to look.

"Next time you're up the trees could you please bring me some more plums?" she asked.

"Okay," us boys said, smiling sheepishly.

Miss Foote told us to have a good day, said goodbye and closed the door.

"She's nice, eh?" Vincent said, as we walked away.

It was clear to me then that I had competition. Vincent wanted to marry Miss Foote, too.

A Short Story

Miss Foote walked into the classroom after morning tea one day holding the latest batch of our handwritten stories. I could tell from the expression on her face that she wasn't happy. She placed the stories down on a desk at the front of the room and looked around at all of us.

"I've had enough," she said to the class. "I want more from you. More from each and every one of you."

Miss Foote addressed the girls first.

"Girls," she said. "I've had enough of stories about fairylands, marshmallow trees, lemonade rivers and ponies. Give me something more."

Miss Foote then turned her attention to us boys.

"Boys," she said. "I don't want to read any more stories about war, about guns and tanks. Give me something more."

I sat at my desk looking at Miss Foote, remembering how much I wanted to marry her. I wanted to write a story that would impress her. A story that she would love. A story that she would never forget. As I watched Miss Foote I thought to myself:

'What sort of things do you like, Miss? What would you like to read about?'

Then it came to me. I knew the sort of things that Miss Foote liked. I took out my pad and my pencil and I wrote a story, a descriptive story about a man taking a walk through a park.

The story described what the man saw as he walked along the path. The birds, the trees, the flowers. The story talked about the man seeing families together, someone walking their dog, someone feeding ducks at a pond, some people having a picnic. It was a simple story. It spoke of the blue sky, the clouds, the sun.

The story finished with the man coming out of the

park to where he could see the ocean. I put on my last full stop, got up from my chair and walked over to my teacher's desk. Miss Foote was sitting there marking our maths books. She saw me approaching.

"Just put your story there please, Timothy," she said, pointing to a pile of books on the side of her desk.

I put my story on the top of the pile and walked back to my desk. I was feeling pretty confident that Miss Foote was going to like my work. Then I forgot all about it, because I was a kid and there were too many other things to think about.

The next day at school Miss Foote walked up to the front of the class. She looked at me.

"Timothy, come up to the front," she said.

My heart sank. What had I done wrong now? What was I in trouble for this time? The last thing that I wanted to do was to let Miss Foote down.

I got up from my chair and started to walk up to the front, and as I did so my mind was going over the last 24 hours, trying to remember what I had done wrong.

At the front I stood behind Miss Foote. Everyone

in the class was looking at me. I dropped my head and shuffled my feet not knowing where to put my gaze.

Miss Foote then read my story out loud to the class.

My face burnt red. Was my writing that bad that the other students had to hear it?

Once Miss Foote had finished reading my story she held it up high.

"This is the sort of writing that I want," she said.

She looked at me and in front of everybody she said, "Well done, Timothy, this is wonderful work, excellent."

I was confused. I only wrote the story to impress her, I didn't think that it was worthy of any fuss. I was just hoping for a pat on the head and a smile.

Miss Foote started to walk away.

"Come with me please, Timothy," she said, her hand outstretched to me.

'I'll go anywhere with you, Miss,' I thought to myself as I went with her.

Miss Foote took me to other classes in the school and my story was read aloud and held up as an example of exceptional writing. I think Miss Foote was partly doing it to prove to the other teachers that Timothy Tipene wasn't a lost cause.

I hadn't been good at anything at school and all of a sudden I was good at something.

I loved and adored Miss Foote so much that I

believed everything that came out of her mouth. If Miss Foote had told me that the sky was purple, then in my mind the sky would be purple. So when Miss Foote told me that I was a writer, not just a writer but a good writer, I believed her. I believed her so much that I never stopped writing.

I had terrible spelling, messy handwriting, and my sentences were usually around the wrong way, but I never gave up. I remain grateful for having Miss Foote as a teacher.

Once Vincent and I knew where Miss Foote lived we were always hanging out around her house, just on the chance that we might get to see her.

One day when Vincent and I were up the plum trees eating plums a car slowed down as it drove past. We watched the car turn into our teacher's driveway. Vincent and I knew what our teacher's car looked like, and that was not her car. The two of us studied the vehicle as it went up the driveway and parked in front of Miss Foote's house.

A man got out.

Vincent and I climbed down from the plum trees. We stood underneath with our hands on our hips.

"Who's that fella?" I asked.

"I don't know," Vincent said. "What's he doing here?"

"That's our teacher!" I groaned.

That man married Miss Foote, and at the end of the year they moved away. My heart was broken.

Miss Foote was at our school for one year, and I was lucky because I got to be in her class. Sadly I didn't get to marry her.

As an adult I haven't found Miss Foote yet, but I'm looking. I would just like to thank her for the difference that she made to me and my life.

THE BATTLESHIP

One afternoon I was in my bedroom when I overheard Shaun and his mate, Stephen, talking outside. They were talking about a battleship at school.

I was nine years old and I was thinking to myself, 'Battleship? There's no battleship at school. If there was a battleship at school I would know.'

So I walked outside and asked my brother and his mate, "What are you talking about?"

"We're talking about our teacher," Shaun said. "Her name's Mrs Battersby. She's real mean and tough. So we call her The Battleship."

"Whoa," I said. "Do you say that to her face?"

Shaun and Stephen both flinched.

"No!" they gasped. "You never say that to her face!"

Shaun looked at me.

"Don't you say it, Timmy," he said, pointing at me.

A few days later it was three in the afternoon. The bell had gone and it was home time. Students were all lined up to go on the buses to go home and Mrs Battersby was on bus duty. She was making sure that we got on the buses in an orderly fashion.

I was the last person to get on the bus. When I got on the bus I saw my uncle, the bus driver. It was always nice to see my uncle. I walked down the bus aisle. There were no more free seats. I had to stand.

My uncle started the bus engine and closed the bus door. Mrs Battersby turned and started to walk back into the school. My uncle slowly moved the bus forward.

I thought that I'd be funny. So I yelled out:

"See ya, Battleship!"

The kids on the bus gasped and looked at me.

Mrs Battersby turned around. "Stop that bus!" she cried.

To my horror my uncle stopped the bus. I shook my head. "Don't stop the bus, Uncle," I cringed. "Don't stop the bus."

The door opened. Mrs Battersby came up the stairs. "Who said that?" she growled.

Everyone looked at me. My face burnt red. Had I really said it so loud?

"Get off this bus now!" Mrs Battersby demanded.

I walked down the aisle. When I went past my brother and his mate sitting in their seats, they were both looking at me.

"You be quiet, Timmy," Shaun muttered. "Don't you tell her that we told you that name."

"Yeah, be quiet Timmy," Stephen added.

I kept walking. Then I saw my uncle. He was grinning at me as if to say, "You're on your own with this one, boy." I climbed down off the bus. Mrs Battersby took me to the side and made me face her.

"Who told you that name?" she asked.

I looked up over her shoulder. I could see back onto the bus where Shaun and Stephen weren't sitting down any more. They were standing up at the window and shaking their heads with a finger to their lips. Then Shaun held up his fist and began punching it into the palm of his other hand.

"C'mon," Mrs Battersby said. "Who told you that name?"

"Shaun and Stephen," I said.

Mrs Battersby got back on the bus.

"Shaun! Stephen!" she cried. "Out here now please!"

The boys glared at me as they got off the bus. Then the three of us got a big telling off in front of all the other kids. My uncle was still grinning when we got back on the bus.

A couple of years later I ended up in Mrs Battersby's class and I was to find that there was a bit more to this Mrs Battersby.

MRS BATTERSBY

Year 7 / Form 1

One day at school I was sitting on the mat with the other children waiting for Mrs Battersby, to arrive. With nothing to do, I studied a boy sitting in front of me. This boy's name was Christopher, and he was different from me. Christopher always wore nice clothes to school. He always had nice lunches. He was a very popular boy, lots of kids liked him, and in the classroom, Christopher tried really hard and was very clever. Even as I was watching him he was sitting up tall with his arms crossed, waiting for Mrs Battersby.

Christopher noticed me looking at him and turned.
"What?" he asked.
"Nothing," I said, looking to the front of the class.

Christopher went back to sitting up straight with his arms crossed, and I went back to watching him.

Christopher turned around again.

"What are you looking at?" he frowned. I was serious.

"Does your dad hit you?" I asked.

"Eh?" Christopher's frown deepened.

"Does your dad hit you?" I repeated.

Christopher was confused.

"What do you mean?" he said.

"You know, hit you?" I replied, demonstrating a punch with my fist.

"No!" Christopher gasped. "My dad would never do that to me." He was horrified at the idea. He looked at me. "Does your dad do that to you?" he queried.

"Yeah," I nodded.

I lifted up my shirt and showed Christopher a large lump in the pit of my left arm.

"My dad punched me really hard in the shoulder and now this big lump has come up," I said.

I was worried. With the lump my body was

changing. I didn't know what was happening. I was thinking that another arm was trying to grow out or something.

"Do you have a lump like that under your arm?" I asked.

"No!" Christopher exclaimed.

"Do you think that lump's supposed to be there?" I queried further.

"No!" Christopher replied, shaking his head. "That's not right. You should tell someone about that. You should tell Mrs Battersby."

"No, no!" I growled, pulling my shirt down to hide the wound. "Don't tell anybody, don't tell anyone."

Mrs Battersby stepped in front of the class and we moved on with our work.

A little later the bell rang. It was morning tea. Us kids went outside, had something to eat and a play.

When the bell rang again we went back to class. I walked in, sat at my desk and watched other children come in and take their seats.

I kept watching, looking out the windows and

through doors for the children approaching. There was no sign of Christopher. I looked around wondering where he was.

'He wouldn't tell anyone about my lump,' I thought to myself. 'I told him not to.'

Soon every student was back, seated at their desk. Every student except Christopher. I could feel my heart beating fast against my chest.

The door from the adjacent class opened. Mrs Battersby walked in, and behind her walked Christopher.

I suddenly found it hard to breathe. I knew straight away that Christopher had told her.

Mrs Battersby looked at me.

"Timothy," she said. "Come with me, please."

I cringed, got up from my desk and started to follow Mrs Battersby and Christopher out of the classroom. I was certain that I was in a whole lot of trouble. I needed a way out.

'Lie,' I thought. 'I'll lie. I'll say that I don't know what Christopher's talking about Miss, he's making up stories. I never said that.'

I had it set in my mind that I was going to lie.

I followed Mrs Battersby and Christopher into the cloakroom. When I got there Mrs Battersby made me stand up against the wall. The teacher and my classmate just stood there watching me. I shuffled about not knowing where to look.

"Lift up your shirt," Mrs Battersby said.

"Eh?" I frowned, suddenly having no ears.

"Timothy, lift up your shirt," Miss Battersby firmly directed.

I sighed. There was no way that I was getting out of this.

I lifted my shirt.

Mrs Battersby saw the lump and the bruising. She looked at me and then burst into tears. Not quiet tears either, but big, loud wailing. Mrs Battersby wrapped me up in her big arms and hugged me.

Mrs Battersby was not a little woman. Mrs Battersby was a big woman, so when she hugged me she engulfed me. At this point I was feeling two things.

Firstly, I felt really uncomfortable. Mrs Battersby

was squeezing me and rocking back and forth as she sobbed. Her tears washed down wetting the side of my face and wetting my shirt.

The second thing that I felt was a voice rising up inside of me. This voice was saying, 'It's not right. Tim. What's happening at home is not right.'

That voice never went away.

Then the worst thing happened.

Mrs Battersby stepped back from me.

"Timothy," she said, wiping her tears. "I want you to go back into the classroom. I want you to pick up your desk, and I want you to put your desk next to mine."

"Eh?" My heart plummeted.

How was putting my desk next to Mrs Battersby's going to help me? That just meant that Mrs Battersby would see that I didn't do any work! That I didn't even know how to do the work! I was being punished.

Dropping my head I banged my way back into the class. The other children watched as I picked up my desk and carried it across the room.

They were like, 'Whoa, Timothy must be in so much trouble.'

I put my desk down beside Mrs Battersby's. I sat in my seat, bent over my desk and buried my face into my arms to hide from the world. When Mrs Battersby re-entered the classroom she was still wiping away her tears. She sat down at her desk and peered over at me.

"Are you all right there, Timothy?" she asked.

I raised my head and nodded.

I then took, 'the position'.

The position was what I used to keep teachers away. I would hunch over my desk, place my left arm around my work to cover it so that no one could see. I would then put my head down close to my left arm and with my right hand I would move my pen to look busy. I had no idea what I was doing when it came to schoolwork, but all I had to do was appear to be doing it.

Through this position my message to teachers was, 'Move along, there is nothing to see here. Just move along. I'm too busy working to disturb. Go and deal with the noisy kids on the other side of the classroom. Just leave me alone!'

Whenever a teacher looked in my direction I would drop into 'the position'.

Mrs Battersby liked to scan the classroom from her desk. Throughout the day she would run her eyes over the class making sure that every student was doing what they were supposed to be doing. She would always start from the left and her gaze would travel all the way around to the right and end with me.

I had to stay sharp and be aware of this so that I didn't get caught out. If I wasn't careful Mrs Battersby would catch me looking out the window or daydreaming off into space. However since Mrs Battersby had seen the lump under my arm she had taken a special interest in me.

"How are you going there, Timothy?" she asked one day.

"Good, good," I said, looking at her briefly and then dropping into 'the position' and moving my pen wildly.

I could feel Mrs Battersby watching me.

"Bring me your book so that I can have a look at your work," she said.

I froze.

The pretence was over. Mrs Battersby would see that I wasn't doing any work.

I sighed, got up from my desk, took my maths book and dropped my head as I stumbled over to Mrs Battersby.

Mrs Battersby took my book, laid it out on her desk in front of her and smoothed it out like it was something precious. She put an arm around me and pulled me in close. Mrs Battersby then gently took me through my work, helping me to understand what I didn't understand.

I could feel my tension slipping away.

'This isn't so bad,' I thought to myself.

I was lucky. I was a 10-year-old boy, and I had a Battleship on my side.

MRS BATTERSBY RETIRES

At the end of the year Mrs Battersby retired. On the last day some of the girls got together and they made Mrs Battersby a pretty card. They let everyone in the class sign the card, everyone except me. I went up to sign the card, but the girls wouldn't let me.

"You're not signing our card," one girl said. "You're a naughty boy and Mrs Battersby doesn't like naughty boys."

I felt angry. In my hand I had a large rubber doorstop. I had found it lying on the ground outside and had been holding onto it all day. When the girls would let everybody else sign the card for Mrs Battersby but not me, I felt angry. So I threw the doorstop as hard as I could up at the wall.

However the doorstop didn't just hit the wall and bounce off. It went into the wall making a big hole.

"Whoooooaaa!" the children all chorused.

"You're going to be in so much trouble," one of the girls said. "Wait till Mrs Battersby sees that."

When Mrs Battersby entered the classroom the girls ran up to her.

"Mrs Battersby, Mrs Battersby," they said. "Look what Timothy did."

They pointed out the hole in the wall.

Mrs Battersby looked at the hole, then looked at me.

I dropped my head. This was not how I wanted Mrs Battersby to remember me. She had been so nice to me and I had let her down.

"Timothy, come here," Mrs Battersby said.

As I walked up to Mrs Battersby all the children were watching. They were like, 'man, he's going to get it from the Battleship.'

But what did Mrs Battersby do? She hugged me and cried.

The other kids were dumbstruck. They looked up at the hole and then back at Mrs Battersby holding me.

"But he put a hole in the wall?" one girl argued.

Mrs Battersby was too busy hugging me to care. She was crying and I was crying. I never wanted to let go of her.

I would miss Mrs Battersby. Just like Mrs Leonard and Mrs Foote, another angel had come into my life for a time, and then was gone.

Without such adults I would never have known love.

Over the years I have been in contact with Mrs Battersby. She is very proud that one of her students has become an award-winning author and created the Warrior Kids programme for children. Mrs Battersby remembers the two of us hugging and crying outside the classroom when she saw the lump under my arm. I am most grateful for her caring and generosity. She changed my life.

*The author with Yvonne Battersby,
aka Mrs Battleship, in 2017*

DAD

Dad saw himself as DIY guy. Whenever there was a manual job around the home that needed doing Dad gave it a go. Sadly for Dad it rarely worked out. Most of what Dad tried to fix never worked again, but that didn't deter him from giving it a go.

"Timmy!" he yelled angrily one morning.

Angry was the only way that Dad spoke to me.

I came downstairs and followed him into the garage. I was thinking that he was wanting me to assist him with something. I dreaded assisting Dad. It wasn't some father-son-time thing. There was a reason that it was me assisting him and not Shaun or Katie.

Whenever Dad tried to fix something and it didn't

work, he'd become enraged and lash out. If the nail he was hammering bent, or the wood broke or the spanner slipped he would swear and hit out at me with whatever he had in his hand at the time. I got very good at evading attacks. The hits that I could never evade were the ones where Dad and Mum were telling me to stand still and take them.

On this particular day, Dad was in a fouler mood than usual. In the garage he went over to the roller door, reached down, took hold of the handle and forcefully wrenched it up. The tin door banged and rattled as it flew up and rolled into a coil. Dad stood beneath it with his hands on his hips glaring angrily out at the world.

With all the force the roller door kept rolling. It rolled right out of its holdings and dropped. It landed directly on Dad's head and then fell backwards crashing onto the concrete floor behind him. Through the whole ordeal Dad didn't move. He just stood there with his hands on his hips. He glanced back at the roller door which now had a large dent in the centre of it from where it had hit his head.

Dad looked back out at the world. Behind him, I struggled to contain my laughter. I knew that the heavy garage door landing on his head must have hurt, but Dad was too staunch to show any pain. I don't know who he was trying to look tough for. The only thing in front of him was a paddock with sheep in.

"Forget it," Dad said, sending me back inside.

There was no work that day. Dad went and lay down instead.

In many ways Dad was a tragic comedy. He worked hard to appear successful, but would then sabotage himself. He bought himself a fancy car, a Mitsubishi Sigma with a turbocharged engine. He was so proud of that car. Problem was, Dad liked his alcohol just as much and the Sigma would always end up in a ditch somewhere. One night Dad was so drunk that he got into his car outside the Grand Hotel in Helensville, turned on the engine and

then fell asleep behind the wheel with the car in park, and his foot pushing the accelerator flat to the floor. Dad's mates tried to get into the car as the engine screamed. However, in his drunkenness Dad had activated the central locking. Eventually they smashed a window to get in, but it was too late. Dad had burnt the engine out. And that isn't the end of the story. After getting the Sigma repaired Dad brought it home cleaned and polished as though it was brand new. He proudly drove it up the driveway with the stereo blaring. He parked the car at the top of the driveway, where he left the engine running to allow the turbo to cool as he walked inside.

Suddenly Mum cried out from the kitchen. Dad had failed to apply the handbrake and his car started to roll back down the drive. Dad made a mad dash out of the house. He jumped, trying to clear the fence encasing the deck, but hit it with his legs, crashed over and fell flat on his face on the lawn. There Dad scrambled back to his feet and chased after his car. The car scraped the fence and backed into a tree where it stopped. The newly repaired car was now scratched and dented. Dad sat on the grass with his head in his hands and wept. Mum went out, sat down and put her arm around him.

MUM

Mum collected animals. She touted herself as their champion. There were animals that she rescued, others that she paid a great deal of money for … and some she stole.

When I was 12 and we had just moved to Makarau, Mum took a fancy to someone's pet black goat. One night she got me in the car and drove to where the goat was tied up to a beautifully decorated goat house. Mum told me to untie the goat quietly, so as not to disturb the owners in the nearby house, and then to get the goat into the back of her car.

I thought about the goat's owners and knowing how important pets were to me, I protested. But Mum wasn't leaving without the goat. Doing as I was told I wrestled the goat into the back of Mum's car, while she sat behind the wheel with the engine running, ready for a quick getaway. In the back seat I had to grapple with the goat all the way home.

One morning Mum came out to go to work and found that goat prancing about on the roof of her brand-new company car. She was furious with the scratches and dents, and the little black poos. I guess it was karma. Once wasn't enough, either. That goat was up on that car roof a number of times.

When visitors came to our house Mum would give them the grand tour, showing off her animals and saying how much each one had cost. Mum would also talk of the personal sacrifice and effort she had put into each of the animal's individual care.

In reality though, Mum was quick to get bored with each animal as she constantly found something new to focus on, so her animals would be forgotten and neglected. They would often get out and roam. The goats were the worst. Especially that black goat that Mum had got me to steal from the side of the road. As a shift worker, Dad slept all hours of the day. One afternoon he had not closed the front door properly and woke to find that goat at his bedside, softly nibbling at his face.

That year the farmers in the area were annoyed with our ram, Norton, another one of Mum's pets. The last thing the farmers wanted was a brown ram with an attitude problem in amongst their white ewes. They would turn up at our place with Norton on a trailer. Swearing and cursing, the farmers would tell us to get better control of our animals.

There were loads of brown lambs that year. Our neighbours weren't impressed.

My parents were city farmers. They didn't have a clue.

I CHOSE A GOOD LIFE

One Christmas Eve I awoke busting to go to the toilet, however I could hear noises in the lounge. Being young, I thought that it must be Santa Claus putting presents under the Christmas tree. I had been told that if Santa Claus caught me awake he wouldn't leave any presents and that meant that I would ruin Christmas for everyone. I knew that Mum and Dad would give me a big beating for that!

I really needed to go to the toilet so, after thinking about it, I crouched on the end of my bed and did a poo there. I used the curtains from the nearby window to wipe my bum afterwards. I figured the beating that I would get from pooing on the end of my bed would be far less than the thrashing that I would get for ruining Christmas. When I had finished, I got back into bed and went back to sleep.

Mum was the one who found my poo in the morning. She was furious and my family were disgusted with me. Thankfully, though, I didn't get a beating. Mum said the reason I wasn't getting one was because she and Dad simply didn't have the time. They were too busy getting ready for a visit from my well-to-do uncle and his children, due to arrive at any moment.

Looking back I can see that fear drove my decision to poo on my bed that night. At the time I thought what I had done was very noble. I was the boy who had saved Christmas.

I wet my bed up to the age of 10 out of fear, but it was only once that I pooed on it.

That decision on Christmas Eve, and the many others I was to make over the years, were all drawn from fear; fear instilled in me by my parents. But there is one decision I am extremely proud of – I decided I would **not** be like my Mum and Dad.

Whenever they hurt me or were cruel to me, I would say in my head, 'I am not going to be like you. I'm going to be different.'

I didn't want to grow up hurting people; to not have self-control. I didn't want my own children, or my partner, to be scared of me as I had been for all those years.

My Mum had told me all the time that I would grow up to be a monster and that I would hurt women and children. Many other people thought that I would end up in trouble or in prison. I wanted to prove them all wrong.

RESPECT

My partner is from China and we like to visit our family in Beijing. When we visit, we have a wonderful time with lots of meals with lots of people.

After one lunch a Chinese man looked at me and said, "Your son," pointing at my boy who was 11 at the time. "He listens to you very well. He is very respectful to you."

I nodded, happy to hear the positive feedback.

"Your son must be very scared of you," the man went on to say. "You must hit him a lot."

"Eh?" I frowned, thinking that I must have misheard him. "Pardon? What did you say?" I asked politely.

'Your son,' the man said again. 'He listens to you

a lot, he is very respectful towards you. You must hit him a lot."

I looked at my son.

"Hey son," I said. "Come here. Our friend here wants to know if I hit you," I said, gesturing at the man.

My son thought it was time to be funny. "Uh yeah," he laughed. "My dad hits me all the time."

I sighed and rolled my eyes though I couldn't help but smile. My son likes to play around.

"Seriously," I said. "He wants to know if I hit you."

My son looked at the man and shook his head.

"No," he said. "My dad has never touched me."

The man frowned.

"That's not possible," he muttered. "You are so respectful; you listen so well. Your dad must hit you."

"No," my son replied. "Never."

Thinking that it was a breakdown in our communication the Chinese man turned to my partner and asked her in Mandarin. The two of them spoke for a while and afterwards the man still looked confused.

"Never?" he said in English.

"Never," my partner replied.

"But he is so respectful and behaves so well," the man said, pointing at my boy. The man looked at me.

"How is this possible?" he asked.

"I listen to my son," I said. "I respect him."

I chose to raise my children differently to how I was raised. I chose to have a home that was safe and free of violence and because of this I have two very good children who are excelling in life.

Whenever there is a problem or someone in my family makes a poor choice we talk about it. I spend a lot of time with my son and daughter.

Because I am safe they know that they can talk to me about anything.

CHOICE

I was too traumatised to learn at school. I could never sit still and the only topics that I could ever focus on were writing and art because they allowed me to escape into my imagination. I didn't go to school to learn; I went to get away from home. At 16 my high school didn't know what to do with me. I had asked teachers and staff for help, telling them about the abuse and violence at home, and explaining to them why I was always in trouble. But in those days attitudes were different. They saw me as a problem and it was easier to just kick me out.

When I was expelled from high school there was lots I didn't know. I knew how to use letters but I couldn't recite the alphabet from A to Z. I also didn't know my times tables or how to tell the time on a clock with hands.

For a long time I believed that I was a failure and that I was stupid. However, once I got away from home and lived in a safe place, a place free from abuse and violence, I found that I was actually quite clever. I also found that I had some long-term effects from my abusive childhood.

It was one thing to want to be different from my parents, but it was another thing entirely to actually be different. Feeling anxious and on edge was my normal. I didn't know how to be any other way. I always felt angry and I was scared of losing it; of smashing things and being abusive. I had to work very hard at being a safe man who was in control, and to do that I needed help. I saw counsellors and therapists for years. I did all sorts of courses, like anger management. I even became a counsellor myself and a facilitator of anger management.

As you have read, I did not always make the best choices when I was young. But as I got older I learnt how to be careful with my life and careful of others.

In 1994 I created Warrior Kids, a programme designed to support children by teaching them self-control and showing them how to get on with others, while also teaching martial arts skills, building their confidence and resilience.

I am now the author of 10 books, five of which have won awards, and an inspirational speaker who has talked to audiences throughout the country. Through my journey to attain self-control I have gained numerous black belts and martial arts teaching titles, and I have been inducted into the New Zealand Martial Arts Hall of Fame. I was recognised as a Kiwibank Local Hero and received a medal for my work in the community. Not bad for someone who was kicked out of school.

No matter how hard it has been, how bleak life may look, regardless of what we have been through, we are blessed every morning with a new day, a new beginning. An opportunity to start over and do things differently.

It took a lot of work over many years. It was hard and challenging, yet today my life is far removed from the violence and abuse that I grew up in. I did not hurt women and children, I didn't hurt anyone, and I did not get into trouble or go to prison. I chose to make a difference in people's lives just like some of my teachers did for me.

I am excited about the future.

My hope is that my story will inspire you to choose a good life for yourself. That you will make better choices, choices that will look after you, your loved ones and your community.

Today I have a beautiful loving partner, two amazing and clever children and a safe home. My life is full of love and warmth.

My childhood was scary and damaging, yet I chose to have a wonderful future, and I make that choice every day.

With much love and hope,
Tim

HELPLINES

If the stories in this book have made you feel that you need more information or would like to talk to someone use the following helplines.

If there is immediate danger phone the police on 111.

- Youthline   Phone: 0800 376 633
  email: talk@youthline.co.nz or free text to 234

- 0800 Kidsline   Phone 0800 543 754

- 0800 What's Up   Phone 0800 942 8787

- The Lowdown – Straight up answers for when life sucks email team@thelowdown.co.nz or free text 5626

Dealing with family violence

- Shine – Making homes violence free Phone 0508 744 633
- Family Violence It's Not Ok   Phone 0800 456 450

For Parents wanting support

- Parent Help   Phone 0800 568 856

ABOUT THE AUTHOR

Tim Tipene overcame a violent and abusive childhood, and broke the cycle to become a renowned inspirational speaker, award-winning author and the founder of the acclaimed Warrior Kids programme.

Tim was adopted and raised in two cultures, NZ Māori and NZ European.

His tribal affiliations are Ngāti Kuri and Ngāti Whātua.

Tim is the author of 10 books, 5 of which have won awards, including the picture books for children, *Māui – Sun Catcher*, *Hinemoa te toa*, *Taming the Taniwha*, *Haere* and *The Wooden Fish*.

www.timtipene.com